Backyard Wonders 2

written by
Nancy MacCoon

illustrations by
Courtney Watkins

Published by
Vibatorium Publishing
www.vibatorium.com

To purchase this book online:

www.backyardwonders.com

Library of Congress
Control Number 2006925040
ISBN 0-9742495-1-3

First Edition
Printed in China

chapter one

HAVE YOU EVER WONDERED ABOUT BUTTERFLIES?

Butterflies are such fun to watch in a garden, with their lovely colors and graceful flight. They seem to be part of the flowers themselves, as if the petals took wing. There are so many of these beautiful insects that you can find them everywhere. After a rainstorm, you will see them flitting about enjoying the sunshine, circling each other, playing and gathering food.

The monarch butterfly is one of the most interesting butterflies. The first time I saw a monarch butterfly, with its Halloween coloring, it had alighted in a fall display of flowers, bats, and witches. It fitted in so perfectly that I couldn't believe that it was real.

As cold weather approaches, monarchs fly great distances and end up in warmer climates. They ride on the winds that blow south in late fall, just the way you might ride a wave at the beach! When they arrive at their destination, their clustering masses of fluttering orange and black cover the trees. The over-wintering spot could be called "Club Med," a place for rest and recreation. The trip home is complicated because the winds don't help them. It takes several generations to accomplish a complete round trip

In early spring the monarch lays her eggs on the underside of the leaves of the milkweed plant. These little pinhead-sized eggs hatch into striped yellow, black, and white caterpillars that eat and eat and eat.

Each caterpillar changes coats several times. After two or three weeks, the final coat becomes hard and forms a case called a chrysalis (KRIS-a-lis) that becomes its bed. This looks like folded up leaves with gold spots and a gold rim around the top. The Pilgrims, thinking the chrysalis looked like a king's crown, named this butterfly the monarch, another name for one who rules over a kingdom.

In seven to ten days, the caterpillar has become a butterfly! The butterfly crawls out and stretches its wet, wrinkled wings. The whole cycle takes about 30 or 40 days to complete.

Butterflies belong to a large group of insects called

Lepidoptera (Lep-i-DOP-ter-a , which means "scaly winged"). Their four wings are covered with tiny overlapping scales that help them fly and provide the colors you see. If you touch the wing, your fingers would gather a collection of tiny scales that look like dust. Butterflies need these to fly, remember, so it's a good idea not to touch the wings.

Instead of a tongue, butterflies have a tube that curls up when it's not sucking up nectar from flowers. You know the noisemaker you get at birthday parties that uncurls when you blow it? That's the way the butterfly's tongue works.

The monarch is special in another way. It feeds on the milkweed plant, which is poisonous to other creatures. By eating this plant, the monarch develops an awful taste that protects it from birds that might try to eat it.

The viceroy butterfly doesn't feed on milkweed but looks much like the monarch. Because of this, birds won't touch the viceroy. They're afraid it will taste like a monarch.

We can invite butterflies to visit us by planting flowers that they especially like. Or you can watch butterflies enjoy a simple dandelion.

chapter two

HAVE YOU EVER WONDERED ABOUT EARTHWORMS?

Earthworms! Dig a hole in some wet dirt and there they are, squirmy, wiggly, and slimy.

There are many species of earthworms. Some are tiny, some huge, some are grey, some red, yellow or dark brown. There's even a bright blue one in the Philippines.

The pinkish-gray worm in your garden is probably the night crawler with the clumsy name of Lumbricus terrestris (LUM-bri-cus ter-RES-tris). The night crawler did not always live in the United States. It came from Europe with the Pilgrims. Pilgrims brought plants growing in dirt. They also used dirt to add weight to their ships for smooth sailing. Guess who was hiding in the dirt? The night crawler!

As with all earthworms, the night crawler's body is divided into segments, as many as 150 in some species. Each segment has a function. The first is the head, where its mouth is. The best way to find the head is to notice the direction the worm is going. If you look very closely, you'll see that the tail end has a flattened shape.

The earthworm's body parts are very simple. Worms have no eyes or ears but their skin is sensitive to light, touch, and outside movement. There are five hearts, a nerve cord, and a special tube to take in food. Do you know what earthworms eat? Dirt! Can you imagine eating dirt all day long? Most of us have made mud pies and maybe even tasted them, but we are not built to eat dirt, and the worms are.

Worms don't use all of the dirt though – the extra bits of dirt that get pushed out are called "castings." These castings are good fertilizer, helping plants to grow. When they dig in the dirt, worms create little tunnels that loosen the soil and let in the oxygen. In fact, you could say that worms are little tunneling farmers.

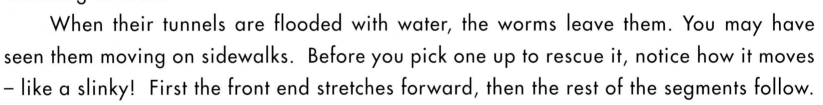

When their tunnels are flooded with water, the worms leave them. You may have seen them moving on sidewalks. Before you pick one up to rescue it, notice how it moves – like a slinky! First the front end stretches forward, then the rest of the segments follow.

Each segment has four pairs of bristles that act like little feet to help it crawl. If you run your finger along the side of a worm, you can feel tiny, stiff bristles. If you move your finger very gently along its back, it will stretch up to meet the stroking.

You can see a slight thickening of skin near the head. This

is the earthworm's cocoon, or baby case. When eggs are stashed there, the cocoon slips over the head of the worm and into the soil.   Several miniature worms are hatched in about three weeks.

Worms can live up to 15 years. Some don't live that long because they get eaten first!

But nature does its best to help them.   I watched a bird try to pull a worm from the ground. The worm resisted. They had a tug-of-war going.   The bird was startled and nearly landed on its tail when it got only the front part of the worm.   Don't worry! Many species of earthworms grow a new head or tail.

Also, worms put little doors on their tunnels to hide from birds. The doors are made with grass and leaves. If you really look, you'll see little tufts of foliage sticking up here and there in your garden.

Perhaps after studying earthworms, you can agree with the ancient Chinese who called them "angels of the earth."

chapter three

HAVE YOU EVER WONDERED ABOUT ANTS?

You can watch little black ants scurry everywhere – near sticky stuff, near water, and in places where you don't want them – like your lunch.

How do they find the food? Scouts go out from the colony. Once they've found their meal by smelling it, they guide their friends to it with a chemical trail, like invisible breadcrumbs. Their friends use their antennae to smell the chemical trail.

If you set up your own feeding station, you can see ants talking together. Draw a circle with a thick line of sidewalk chalk with an opening for an entrance near a group of ants. Place a piece of protein in the center of the circle. (I used bacon bits.) As soon as the ants find the food, you'll see them wiggling and touching each other's antennae. They go crazy! The number of ants in your circle quickly doubles and the food begins to disappear. The chalk contains most of the activity because ants don't like to cross the chalk line.

Sometimes water running in the garden will flood an ant colony.   You might see a

train of ants clearing out their home, fleeing with eggs and larvae clutched in their mouths (or mandibles).

Ants are insects of the same order as bees and wasps, Hymenoptera (Hy-men-OP-ter-a). They have their own family, Formicidae (For-MISS-I-dee).

There are many varieties of ants. Ants can be smaller than 1/16th

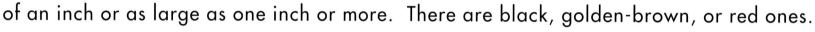

of an inch or as large as one inch or more. There are black, golden-brown, or red ones.

Ants live in a well-developed colony with thousands of members. The queen usually starts a colony by digging a tunnel straight down and then hollowing out a room. The queen might have a morsel of food with her, a fungus (FUN-gus) that she farms. (A mushroom is a fungus, for example; so is mold.) She lays fertilized eggs that develop into her adult daughters with certain jobs to do. There are nurses that care for the new eggs and babies. Cleaners use special wastebaskets for

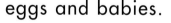

the garbage and take it out. Farmer type ants harvest seeds or tend the fungus crop. Workers search for food, and soldiers defend the colony. The males, sons of the queen, are produced from unfertilized eggs just in

time for the mating season.

The soldiers can tell by smell and looks whether an ant is a stranger. If it's a stranger, the scout will quickly fight. With some of the stranger's chemical on her, she will race back to the colony and alert others of the danger. The smell and the chemical trail she has spread tell the tale. Her soldier comrades rush out, kill the invader, and save the colony. This organized army can defeat even quite large enemies, like lizards.

Some ants use aphids as their cows. Aphids are the tiny green, gold, or black creatures that live on rose bushes and other plants. Ants "milk" sweet fluid from the aphids by stroking them.

Leafcutter ants are fun to watch because they harvest leaves and carry the pieces, like small umbrellas, back to their colony.

A friend of mine lost her contact lens. She found it because she saw it moving in the arms of a very tiny ant. Do you suppose the ant was taking this huge crystal bowl as a gift to the queen?

For creatures that are so small, the ants' strength comes from working together with a well-developed plan. Each ant knows her job and does it well. Even though an ant's brain is very tiny, a large colony of 40,000 ants will have as many brain cells as one human.

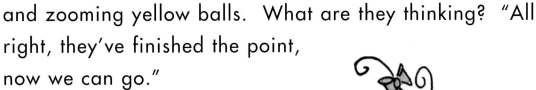

chapter four

HAVE YOU EVER WONDERED ABOUT SPARROWS?

In our neighborhood we have what I like to call "Tennis Court Sparrows." They build their nest in the eaves on the south end of the tennis court. Flying about collecting grass, they seem to ignore the presence of tennis players and zooming yellow balls. What are they thinking? "All right, they've finished the point, now we can go."

I climbed up to look at the nest and discovered that the birds had collected the yellow tennis ball fuzz from the corners of the tennis court. It made a nice cushion for their eggs. I couldn't stay long because the parents came back. They flew at me, poking

me with their sharp beaks and noisily flapping their wings, squawking that I was trespassing!

The male and female sparrows take turns sitting on the nest to keep the eggs warm. There are usually five grape-sized eggs in the nest. After ten or fourteen days, the babies peck their way out of the egg and their gaping mouths signal their hunger.

One little newly hatched bird, featherless and pink, fell out of its nest. We put it back. It fell out again. We put it back again. It was so new that its bones were soft and squishable, so it seemed to survive such a catastrophe. But the parents had to be frightened that their baby had a human smell. And, yes, they have noses that detect such smells.

The parents hunt for food and feed the nestlings for the next sixteen days. Then, the babies learn to fly and become fledglings. Sparrows are probably the most common bird in the world. There are many kinds and it might take an expert to tell the difference between the house sparrow and others. They are part of the huge group of

#1 SPARROW

perching birds, Passerformes (Pas ser FORM es). These birds are suited to perch or grab hold of a branch or wire with three toes that point forward, one that points back. Look at your own hand when you hold a ball. Four fingers point forward, your thumb points back. Your thumb makes it possible to grab hold of things. That's like the bird's foot. There are more birds in this group than in any of the other bird groups. They have adapted to their surroundings very well and have thrived. They like buildings because of the shelter and height. That's why these sparrows are called House Sparrows, not really Tennis Court Sparrows.

When you see these stocky little birds, you will note their brown backs with black streaks and chestnut red shoulders with white streaks. The male bird is more colorful than the female. Chances are the birds flitting about the tennis court make up a community that stays the same over the years.

Watch birds fly. Some flap regularly, some flap and soar and glide. Their wing size and strength have adapted to spaces and air currents available. Sparrows live in smaller areas, with cramped flying and fast turning. They don't glide. All birds use their flying feathers to push the air. These feathers have little hooks (a bit like Velcro) on them so the feathers are connected to each other to allow efficient flying. If you are pushing

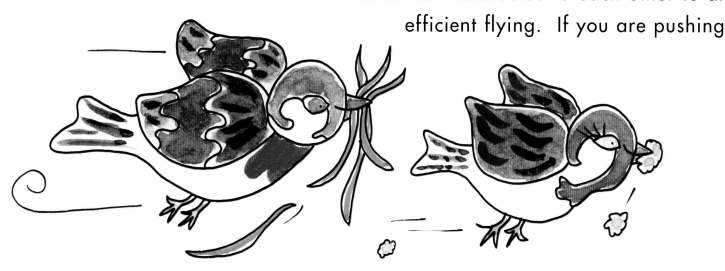

your hand through water, you can move the water better if your fingers are close to each other.

You have heard about the label "birdbrain," meaning not very smart. I have a surprise for you. Birds have very well developed brains. They might hide a seed, see another bird, and sneak back to put it somewhere else. We watched sparrows pick up pebbles on a rooftop, carry them, one by one, to the edge and drop them. They would turn their heads to hear the sound of the dropping pebble. Did they laugh as you do when you toss a coin down a well and listen for the final splash?

chapter five

HAVE YOU EVER WONDERED ABOUT SNAILS?

Here's another slinky, slimy creature for us to talk about, the snail.

Other than the slimy part, they don't resemble the earthworm at all. They come from the group called Mollusks (MOL-lusks) and are related to clams and octopuses.

A snail is called a gastropod, (GAS-tro-pod) which means stomach foot. You see it sliding along on that foot, carrying its home on its back. All its important body parts are in its house, the circular shell. The leading end of the foot is the snail's head with two sets of antennae: a longer pair holds the eyes, the shorter pair acts as nose and finger tips.

The mouth is up front also. There is one jaw on top and a jagged, toothy tongue that grates the food against the jaw. You can tell it likes green leaves from all the holes in the plants in the garden.

We've been talking about a snail as an "it." It's actually both male and female. However, they do need a partner for mating and there is a sort of courtship. Since we know how slowly snails move, you probably couldn't tell that they circle around and touch each other. It might take several hours. About 85 or more eggs are laid fairly soon thereafter. They are buried in a nest about two inches

below the surface of the soil. The eggs look like a heap of small white pearls.

The new little snails hatch in two to four weeks, depending on the weather. They like it moist and warm. The newly hatched snail shells have only one coil or spiral. The pattern is a miniature of the adult shell. The young snail grows and the edge of the shell is made larger by adding another spiral below the last one. A snail is fully adult in eight months.

You'll see a track behind a snail that appears to be silvery and slippery. This is made by a form of mucous, much like egg white, which protects the soft underside and allows the snail to move over sharp territory or even a razor blade. The snail's foot can curl around a twig and hold on. Quite often you'll notice a snail has climbed up a window. Since their movement is usually toward food, what do you suppose it thinks is up there? It must have taken it "forever" to arrive at that spot. Do you feel sorry for it? All that wasted determination?

Snails have an interesting defense against enemies, particularly ants. They let loose a bubbly foam which glues the enemies together.

If you are fond of finger plays, like "Itsy, bitsy spider," you would find it difficult to do one for snails.

"Here comes a snail, it's crawling up the stair.
Its shell is its home it carries everywhere.
After many hours, one stair is all it's done.
Our snail is busy working but is it any fun?"

Have you moved your hands at all? No, I didn't think so.

When I started studying snails, I began to have problems with getting rid of them when they were chewing my flowers. I couldn't step on these beautiful shells. Finally, since the snail is a delicious treat to birds, I began tossing the snails up at the sleek black crows sitting on the telephone lines. Soon, it seemed, the crows were waiting for their flying dinner.

chapter six

HAVE YOU EVER WONDERED ABOUT SQUIRRELS?

Have you ever seen squirrels chase each other? I watched two squirrels run up a tall pine tree, going around and around the trunk. It didn't seem as if they were trying to catch each other. It was more of a game of tag for these slender, furry little creatures.

One of them raced across a branch onto a telephone wire and dashed across. The other one followed.

How do squirrels run on a wire and not lose their balance? By going fast. If they stop, they'll fall off. Also their tail helps them balance. If they do fall, their tail slows them down. The squirrel's family name is Sciuridae (SI-yoo-ri-dee) which means

shade tail. Would you choose "parachute tail" instead?

One day sitting at a table in my garden, I was reading and eating nuts from a plastic bag. One squirrel liked the smell of my nuts so I named her "Nutty." She was full of personality. Chattering and playful, she used her tail as an exclamation point, a switch here, and swipe there. She scouted my nuts with her nose wiggling. She sneaked closer and finally jumped up on the table. I could see her hand-like paws with long fingers and curved claws. Fearlessly, Nutty snatched the bag of nuts and zoomed off the table.

The next time I was outside, I kept my nuts safe by putting them in a plastic box with a lid. But Nutty managed to bite through that thick plastic before I noticed. Sneaky!

Squirrels are rodents. The word "rodent" comes from the Latin word "to gnaw" which means "to bite or chew on." All rodents have long front teeth that never stop growing. They keep their teeth short and sharp by gnawing on things. Squirrels' jaws and front teeth are good at biting and cutting. Their back teeth grind up the cut food.

Since Nutty loved my nuts, I set up a feeding station with peanuts in our tree. Nutty and the other squirrels loved eating those nuts. They'd sit nearby, crunch the shells, and eat the nuts. Sometimes they'd take two or three nuts and bury them in the garden, wherever the earth was soft enough for digging. Squirrels don't always remember where they put them, though, so they use their nose to find them. Perhaps in a field somewhere, Nutty has hidden a few nuts that she will never find. These nuts might grow into big trees.

Nutty also liked the green pinecones from our tree. I watched her eat a pinecone the same way we would eat corn-on-the cob. She sat upright and turned the cone with her hands.

Did you know squirrels have whiskers? Just like other animals with whiskers, squirrels use theirs to measure things. "Is that tree hole wide enough for me?" There are squirrels of different sizes, from mouse-sized to cat-sized. They come in various colors, too: black, grey, brown, reddish, even albino, and often in a combination of colors. Nutty is a fox squirrel, with a light tan tummy and a grayish coat. She looked funny when she ate the blossoms of the bottlebrush tree. She had an extra set of bright red whiskers.

In the springtime and sometimes again in the fall, squirrels produce their pups, usually four or five, after about five weeks of pregnancy. The pups are pink and hairless. Their eyes are closed until they are 30 days old. Their mother nurses them for nearly 10 weeks. Their father doesn't help at all. Squirrels can live for six or seven years; some even live as long as eighteen years.

They have lots of different homes. Some live in forests and others live in parks. Some may even live in your own backyard. If you see a mass of twigs high up in a tree, it might be a squirrel nest. They also like pine trees, tree hollows, or the fork of a tree. They use shredded bark, leaves, twigs,

and whatever soft material they can find for the nest. They will even use lint from a clothes dryer!

You might be tempted to want a squirrel for a pet. Just think about those sharp teeth and keep your fingers away from them. Squirrels are wild animals and deserve the freedom to leap from tree branches to rooftops to high wires and chase their furry friends.

THE END

What an interesting book for children! It is a delight for parents (and grandparents), too, to find a good age-level zoology book that is true to nature and answers the very questions children like to ask. I like the fact that you tell the kids scientific names and some real natural history facts. Kids will love this book!

Pat H. Wells, Ph.D.
Professor of Zoology Emeritus
Occidental College, Los Angeles

About the Author Nancy MacCoon
Author, Naturalist & Theatre Producer

A gifted writer, who received her first literary recognition at the age of 10, Nancy MacCoon's first love has always been the theatre. As a young woman, she dreamed of becoming a musical comedy star. Nancy pursued this dream and worked as a stage and TV actress until her acting career was cut short by a hearing loss. It was hard for Nancy to relinquish this dream, but understanding directors hidden behind the camera became impossible.

Starting a family was the next order of business. With two young children, Nancy chose to redirect her efforts into producing children's theater. While this was a dramatic change, it gave her a place to utilize her artistic talents and express herself creatively. Later she wrote the music and lyrics to a play produced by her beloved children's theatre group in Los Angeles, The Nine O'Clock Players. Fast-forward to the 1990's when Nancy, an avid naturalist, was watering her backyard when a hummingbird began drinking from the hose and a sow bug strolled by. In that moment, the concept for Backyard Wonders, a series of books to introduce children to the magical in the everyday was born.

Nancy has a degree in zoology, graduated from the Institute of Children's Literature, and has written for newspapers including The Christian Science Monitor, The Los Angeles Times, and The Larchmont Chronicle. She remains on the staff of The Larchmont Chronicle.

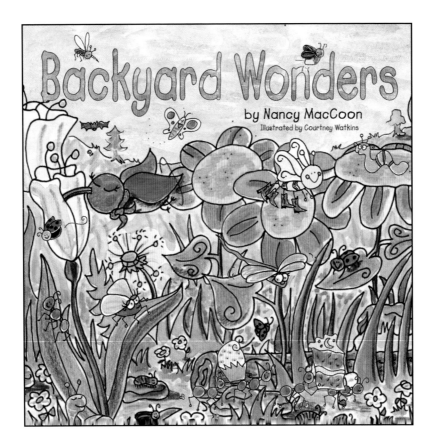

In the first book of the Backyard Wonders series, author Nancy MacCoon describes the personalities of sow bugs, ladybugs, hummingbirds, bumblebees, fireflies, and bats. Hummingbirds flap their wings between 50 and 80 times a second, ladybugs protect themselves by tasting awful, and the sow bugs' family dates back to the dinosaurs.

"Backyard Wonders encourages imagination and curiosity and might be the only nature book where young children both learn and chuckle," says MacCoon. "The book is full of accurate information, whimsical observations, and colorful illustrations. It is written for children age 6 to 10, but appeals to the child in everyone."

Publisher: Vibatorium Publishing (May 2003)
ISBN: 0-9742495-0-5
Suggested retail price: $14.95
Distribution information: www.backyardwonders.com
Email: info@backyardwonders.com